# Chakras

A Beginner's Guide to the
7 Chakras for Balance
and Healing

# Preface

Have you ever wondered what chakras are?

Do you think one of your chakras is blocked?

Do you think chakras have an impact on other aspects of your life?

If you answered yes to any of these questions, this book is for you! Understanding chakras and how they work will allow you to bring more balance into your life as well as teach you about the connections between your body and the energy system.

With this book, you will learn everything you need to know about chakras and how keeping them balanced will impact your life.

# Table of Contents


Preface ................................................................. iii

Introduction .............................................................1

**Chapter 1: The Energy System**..............................3
    The Science behind the Spirit ...............................4
    So How Does It Work Exactly? ...........................4
    What Does It Look Like?.....................................5
    The 7 Main Chakras...........................................7

**Chapter 2: The Seven Chakras** ........................9
    Root Chakra (Muladhara) ..................................9
    Sacral Chakra (Svadhishthana) .........................12
    Navel/Solar Plexus (Manipura Chakra).............15
    Heart (Anahata Chakra) ...................................17
    Throat (Vishuddha Chakra) ..............................19
    Third Eye (Ajna Chakra) ...................................21
    The Crown (Sahastrara Chakra) ........................23

**Chapter 3: Healing and Balancing Chakras**...........26
    Root Chakra (Muladhara) .................................26
    Sacral (Svadhishthana Chakra) .........................28
    Navel/Solar Plexus (Manipura Chakra)..............30
    Heart (Anahata Chakra) ...................................31

Throat (Vishuddha Chakra) ..................................... 32
Third Eye (Ajna Chakra) ......................................... 34
The Crown (Sahastrara Chakra) .......................... 35

**Chapter 4: Chakras and Physical Health** ............... **37**
Root (Muladhara Chakra) .................................... 38
Sacral (Svadhishthana Chakra) ........................... 39
Navel/Solar Plexus (Manipura Chakra) ............. 41
Heart (Anahata Chakra) ...................................... 42
Throat (Vishuddha Chakra) ................................ 43
Third Eye (Ajna Chakra) ..................................... 45
The Crown (Sahastrara Chakra) ......................... 46

**Chapter 5: Chakras and Emotional Well-Being** ..... **50**
Root (Muladhara Chakra) .................................... 51
Sacral (Svadhishthana Chakra) ........................... 53
Navel/Solar Plexus (Manipura Chakra) ............. 55
Heart (Anahata Chakra) ...................................... 57
Throat (Vishuddha Chakra) ................................ 58
Third Eye (Ajna Chakra) ..................................... 60
The Crown (Sahastrara Chakra) ......................... 61

**Conclusion** ............................................................ **64**

**References** ............................................................. **67**

# Introduction

*"There is deep wisdom within our very flesh*
*if we can only come to our senses and feel it."*
Elizabeth Behnke

We often fall victim to our own ambitions. As the human race explores new frontiers such as space, the deepest oceans, and the farthest ends of the Earth, we miss out on exploring the most magical and enigmatic mystery in our ancient and modern history: Ourselves.

*"Our bodies are temples."* The quote sums up the essence of the following pages. By choosing to read on, you will find yourself immersed in the ancient teachings of Hinduism and Buddhism, dating back over 3000 years ago (1500 BC to 500 BC) when this practice is believed to have originated according to the ancient text of Vedas and Tantra.

The elaborate Chakra system is composed of focal points of energy, or Prana Shakti, flowing through our bodies, affecting our minds, physical bodies, and Astral existence.

In this guide, you'll find the hidden meanings of words you hear in Yoga classes and their true impacts on our bodies. We will explore how the Chakras affect us mentally and how they help maintain our intellectual stability. We will dive into their influence on our physical bodies and how they complement modern medicine.

You will find easy step-by-step instructions on opening, balancing, and keeping your Pranas (energy life force) thriving and healthy.

It is easy to feel overwhelmed when looking into a new topic or trying to learn a new skill, especially if you're trying to fit it within your busy day-to-day schedule, and this is why this book has broken down the information you need into bite-sized instructions and easy hands-on methods for beginners combined with a few fun facts for an enjoyable read.

# Chapter 1:

## The Energy System

If we were to walk around the block and ask people what energy means, we would end up with one conclusion: energy means different things to different people.

For some, it's the vibes they get from places and other individuals. For others, it's a flow that makes them feel alive and connects them to nature, while some will refer to it in a spiritual context, a force that guides them through life.

There is no wrong answer — each unique interpretation of this enigmatic unseen power can be cataloged under its definition.

Humans radiate energy like fire from a fireplace full of warmth and light (no, not really, but you get the picture), and we take in energy from other organisms.

But what does that have to do with chakras, you ask? In this chapter, you'll discover the symbiotic relationship between chakras and energy.

## The Science behind the Spirit

The word Chakra, translated from Hindi word for word, means "Wheel of spinning Energy."

A more commonly known definition for it is the "disc" or simply the "wheel," which refers to the wheels in our Astral body that keep the Energy flowing through properly — to maintain our spiritual, physical, and psychological balance.

With the birthplace being Asia, the Energy flow between the chakras is referred to by different names in different cultures. In Sanskrit, it's called "Prana". The Chinese refer to it as "Chi," and the Japanese call it "Qi".

## So How Does It Work Exactly?

Our energy flows outwards, radiating in a spiral form, moving out of our bodies. In that spiraling movement, our chakras, "the wheels that operate the Energy flow," stir in 2 main directions: they operate clockwise to spread our energy to the area and to the people surrounding us, and they flow counter-clockwise to attract and absorb energies from the environment and individuals close to us.

The regularity of each chakras vibrations determines whether we give energy or take it into ourselves.

If the energy between the chakras flows too slowly or fast, you can expect the corresponding Chakra to be a little out of whack, leading to either a physical or mental imbalance that would manifest in our daily lives.

Understanding and visualizing the different flows, strengths, and impacts of this energy will help provide a deeper understanding of each chakra point and how to consciously control its flow. To put it simply, energy and Chakra complement each other; they operate together to keep the body in sync, and the chakras are the instruments and centers of energy. They are receptors that permit us to experience our truth through energy regulation.

## What Does It Look Like?

Now as you may have guessed, there has been some controversy on how energy flow looks and how chakras are shaped.

First, it is invisible and cannot be seen by the naked eye, so most common interpretations are the result of ancient scholars' conscientiousness.

Nevertheless, a common opinion describes the invisible energy as either condensed or subtle, starting from the base of the spine, where the energy is most concentrated, and ending with the top of the spine, where it's more refined and sophisticated.

When visualizing how chakras look, you might want to shed the idea of the rainbow for now. In the ancient teachings, they were described as being in different colors—sometimes without color altogether. Depending on which script you decide to practice from, you will see a contrast of different colors.

Size-wise, there are different approaches; some believe a chakra is a foot wide, some believe they expand and contract according to the energy flow, and in the ancient text, they're described as a small presence within the astral spinal cord that inhabits the physical spinal cord.

While many prefer the customary belief that they are represented as spheres, circles, balls, vortexes, or wheels, others prefer to see them in the form of lotuses – some with the corresponding deity on a set lotus. And there is the belief that each one could have a different shape altogether (square, triangle, crescent moon, hexagram…take your pick!), each with a different representation of color and meaning. Though, to me, the wildest interpretation of all is that it looks like an ice cream cone.

## The 7 Main Chakras

There are 7 well-known chakra points within our bodies, distributed along the spine from the base to the top of the head.

It is proposed that in our entire body, there are around 114 chakra points minor (which are known in Ayurveda as Marma) and major. The Nath Charit, Vijnana Bhairava Tantra, and Shaiva text establish the main chakras as 12 rather than 7. The Siddha-Siddhanta-Paddhati focuses on 9 main chakras, while the Netra Tantra describes 6 (with completely different names than the commonly known ones today).

While it's intriguing and tempting to dive into every single one and explore the lesser-known chakras, we will focus on the more commonly known 7 chakras in this book.

- Root (Muladhara Chakra)
- Sacral (Svadhishthana Chakra)
- Navel/Solar Plexus (Manipura Chakra)
- Heart (Anahata Chakra)
- Throat (Vishuddha Chakra)
- Third eye (Ajna Chakra)
- The Crown (Sahastrara Chakra)

Each Chakra corresponds to a body part in our physical appearance. Each one has its own Mantra and regulates the energy in and out of the area affecting the physical and Astral domain, working through the mind, body, and soul.

If practiced properly and with a conscious mind, they maintain the balance of our being. However, If they are blocked, we experience mental discomfort, ranging from loneliness to greed and insecurities, and physical discomforts such as headaches, aches, pains, or indigestion.

There are different kinds of energies stored within each Chakra. Each one holds our emotions, thoughts, memories, trials, and physical actions. They affect the present and future health of our mind, body, and soul.

Since these Chakras pull Energy from the outside world, they are vulnerable to negative influences that usually manifest in the form of different ailments if they are not kept healthy, balanced, and operating at their best.

As we explore the topic further, we will show how to be aware of each Chakra's functionality and how to reach the equilibrium needed for a healthier existence.

# Chapter 2:

## The Seven Chakras

In this chapter, we dive deeper into each of the 7 main wheels that spin life into our astral selves.

## Root Chakra (Muladhara)

The name Muladhara is derived from Sanskrit, where Mula translates to "root", and adhara translates to "base" or "support."

Similar to its namesake, the Root Chakra enhances the emotions related to home, safety, stability, and connection with the earth. It nourishes the remaining wheels and assists in enhancing their performance.

### Characteristics

This Chakra is linked to the element Earth (Prithvi), and the first Chakra is believed to derive the balance and stability in the remaining six.

As mentioned before, Chakras are invisible; in reality, they have no color, but assigning one to each helps with picturing their effects and directions — sort of like assigning colors to emotions (such as seeing red when angry; you didn't actually see the color red, but it paints the visual of the severity of the emotion).

The color commonly associated with the Muladhara is deep red, which conveniently is also associated with Earth.

It symbolizes Strength and Liveliness and is linked to the elemental emotions of survival.

The main symbol is a four-petaled Lotus viewed in a square shape, an inverted triangle with the Mantra LAM seed in the middle.

There is more than one interpretation for the 4 petals; to some, it symbolizes Ego, Mind, Intellect, and Consciousness. To others, it represents the 4 earthly elements, Earth, Fire Water, and Air.

## Location

The root Chakra is the first of Seven Chakras aligned along our astral spine. It is situated right at the end near the tailbone or Coccyx, which is at the base of the spine (the perineum). A location that allows a solid base for energy flow through all six wheels.

When the Muldhara is balanced, one feels more grounded to the earth and stronger in life. On the other hand, in a state of imbalance, you'd feel lost, agitated, and unsafe.

This location symbolizes the unseen link between the world we exist in physically and the Astral existence.

## An Imbalanced Muladhara

A number of symptoms occur on both fronts, physically and emotionally, when diagnosing an imbalance.

Physical impact includes feeling tired, gaining or losing weight, colon issues, pelvic pain, constipation, sleep depravity, arthritis, and back pain.

Emotionally, you may experience feelings of loss, lack of safety, disassociation, depression, anger, lack of enthusiasm or motivation, financial instability, and hoarding behaviors.

## Healing the Imbalance

Healing and attempting to rebalance a blocked root Chakra allow for a steady and smooth flow of energy through the body, affirming your sense of belonging to the Earth and stabilizing the rest of the vortices.

Following the old teachings, there are a few practical ways to heal, unblock and balance the Muladhara.

- Movement and Exercise
- Meditation

- Yoga
- Breath work
- Root-based foods (Nourishing the body)
- Affirmations

## Sacral Chakra (Svadhishthana)

The Sacral Chakra, also known as the Sex Chakra, is the second of the seven Chakras located along the spine. While the Root Chakra is all about stability and being grounded, the Sacral Chakra is on the other end of the stick, with a focus on movement, flow, and letting go completely.

The Sanskrit name for the second Energy wheel is Svadhishthana, which can be loosely translated into "my own sweet abode," "dwelling place of self," or "where your being is established."

In some beliefs, this Chakra is linked to the Goddess Parvati, the Hindu Deity for fidelity, fertility, and power.

### Characteristics

The Element this Chakra adapts is that of water, "Jala" the Sacral Chakra is responsible for regulating water absorbed in our bodies from food and drink. This energy center thrives on movement and flow like a river remaining clean as long as it flows and regenerates, and adapts the concepts of flow, accepting change and letting go.

It governs our emotions, sensory desires and provides a sense of joy and contentment.

The Svadhisthana is represented by the color Orange. As the water in of itself has no color, this color is derived from the first and third Chakras root (Red) and fire (Yellow), creating the vibrant Orange, which symbolizes the rise and awakening of consciousness.

The symbol of the Sacral Chakra is the crescent moon within a circle within a six-petaled lotus. We can easily find the correlation between the moon and water, where the different phases of the moon affect the tides; this Chakra influences the menstruation cycles women experience, being the home of the Yin energy.

The crescent moon and circle are said to represent death and rebirth, the cycles of life, while the six petals symbolize the negative aspects of our nature – that in order to achieve balance, we must overcome them.

## Location

Some practitioners believe that this Chakra is located in the lower abdomen below the Navel, slightly above the Muladhara, and is linked to the kidneys and sex organs.

## An Imbalanced Svadhisthana

A blockage in the Sacral Chakra can cause emotional disparity – to either be overly emotional and distressed or lack of emotional connection all together.

Some of the physical signs that this Chakra is off-kilter are hip issues, lower back aches, sexual problems, anemia, ovarian cyst, low energy, joint problems, and sinusitis, among other symptoms.

On the emotional front, the side effects range from detachment to the feeling of drowning in one's emotions, fear of pleasure, loneliness, mood swings, addictive behaviors, excessive displays of affection, and others.

## Healing the Imbalance

To unblock and restore balance to the Svadhisthana, we need to release the energy trapped within that area. This can be done through several practices:

- Yoga
- Orange-colored foods
- Affirmations
- Journaling
- Meditation

# Navel/Solar Plexus (Manipura Chakra)

The Manipura is the third Chakra in the Energy system. The Sanskrit name translates to "city of jewels," "Lustrous Gem," or "Place of Shining Gem," linked directly to the third natural element, Fire. This Chakra resembles confidence, learning, a strong sense of self, determination, and what is commonly known as the gut feeling.

## Characteristics

As fire is the element visualized for this Chakra, the sensations associated with it are warmth and light. The Manipura qualities have a sort of fiery nature, like ego, aggression, and willpower. It is also known as the center for energy digestion (Samana Vayu or Samana Prana).

It comes as no surprise that it is the bold hue of yellow. Yellow symbolizes knowledge and intellect, so if you're normally attracted to that color, it likely means you are quite smart.

This Chakra's symbol is a ten-petaled lotus; within it is a yellow circle and a downward-facing triangle symbolizing the tattva of fire.

Each of the ten petals includes Sanskrit lettering, and each letter is translated into the results of an unbalanced Manipura (jealousy, ambition, foolishness, unhappiness, shame, deception, fear, disgust, and spiritual ignorance).

## Location

The Manipura is located in the abdomen, above the Navel (belly button), and close to the spine. It is believed that its energy flows upward from the Navel to the breastbone.

## An Imbalanced Manipura

You may notice your confidence waning somewhat, and you find yourself growing more concerned with what other people think of you or how you're viewed in the public eye when your "gut feeling" is off. You could experience inadequacy or become power-hungry and bossy. Physical side effects include heartburn, ulcers, digestive issues, fatigue, and respiratory problems.

These symptoms point to your Fire Wheel not spinning in the right direction. It is either too fast or too slow.

## Healing the Imbalance

To restore the Fire Chakra, consider the following:

- Yoga
- Meditation
- Affirmations

- Burning incense and oils
- Reflecting on the past and healing from it
- Ingesting yellow-colored foods

# Heart (Anahata Chakra)

The fourth Energy Center and the halfway point of all seven Chakras is the one maintaining love and relationships. The word Anahata in Sanskrit means "Unstruck" or "Unhurt" and sometimes "Pure." The fourth Chakra is the bridge connecting the first three Chakras representing the external world, and the highest three focus on intuition and spirituality.

## Characteristics

The Element that connects to the heart Chakra is Air (Vayu). Air is also associated with touch, expansion, and our connection to emotions. If the Chakra is open, you can express yourself more freely and feel the joy in life, opening yourself to others and maintaining heart health.

This Chakra's color is Green, symbolizing Growth, Love, Healing, and Harmony.

The color green is known to induce calmness and serenity. When you picture green, you see forests, fields, trees, leaves, and organisms that are simply calm, collected, healthy, and in tune with their surroundings.

In some readings, you might find an association with the color pink for Love, but the dominating belief remains that it is Green.

The Anahata symbol is described as two tangled triangles (a hexagram), implying duality within a twelve-petaled Lotus that signals the twelve sounds you hear when this Chakra rotates, engulfed in a green color.

## Location

This energy wheel resides right at the center of the chest beside the heart.

## An Imbalanced Anahata

This Chakra focuses on emotions, love, and attachment, so an imbalance could have you experiencing severe attachment or detachment issues, lack of trust in external relationships, shyness, fear, or adopting a judgmental attitude. Physically, the heart Chakra links to the lungs, thymus glands, upper back, and heart. Therefore, circulation problems, trouble breathing, immune system issues, and back pain, among other symptoms, could occur.

**Healing the Imbalance**

When the heart is wounded, it takes time to patch itself up. The best way to heal this imbalance is to be willing to risk your heart again. That, along with other practical pain-free ways:

- Practicing self-love
- Yoga
- Green foods
- Meditation
- Affirmations
- Aromatherapy

# Throat (Vishuddha Chakra)

Moving up into the highest three Chakras, we arrive at the Throat, also known in Sanskrit as Vishuddha, which means "purifying the body from harmful substances."

The Throat Chakra is all about vocalization, communicating fearlessly to others, and being true to oneself. It also engages with internal communication, body language, and creativity.

## Characteristics

Although some scholars and ancient teachings suggest that the element is the same as its color "Blue"– which is the coolest of colors – others are more inclined to believe it is sound, while some lean towards attaching it to Space (Ether or Akasha).

Invariably, most of them symbolize seeking the truth, stillness, and decluttering the mind from negative thoughts.

The Vishuddha symbol includes a 16-petaled lotus (notice the increase in petals the higher we move along the spine) with an inverted triangle within a circle within it.

## Location

It's located in the throat – specifically the center of the Larynx, which is at the base of the throat. This strategic location links the verbal and body languages in a tight connection.

## An Imbalanced Vishuddha

This imbalance could manifest as a fear of speaking your truth, the inability to listen, as an anxious communicator, gossiping, talking over others, and complaining. Physically, it could show up in hormone fluctuations, neck pain, a sore throat, laryngitis, or thyroid challenges.

## Healing the Imbalance

Let's explore some easy fixes for the lack of balance in the Vishuddha:

- Food for throat (apples, plums, whole grains)
- Meditation
- Yoga
- Affirmations
- Journaling
- Neck and head stretches

## Third Eye (Ajna Chakra)

The third eye is referred to as the eyebrow Chakra or Ajna in Sanskrit, meaning "to perceive," "command," or "beyond wisdom." In Modern practices, it is known as the sixth sense – t intuition and spiritual consciousness, being aware, and the ability to perceive the past and sometimes the future.

It connects the conscious to the subconscious mind and is responsible for sharpening your senses.

### Characteristics

The Ajna Element is Light, enhancing clarity and shedding the darkness clouding our perceptions, taking into consideration that the ancient scripture describes the third eye as being blind.

The color associated with the third eye is indigo or purple, representing freedom of expression and thought. It is the color of inner knowledge and wisdom which enhances the five senses.

For this symbol, there is a shift in the number of petals coming down from the sixteen in the throat Chakra all the way back to only two, engulfing a circle with an upside-down triangle within it. It supports the belief of supreme intellect and spiritual insight.

## Location

This Chakra is situated at the halfway point between your eyebrows. At the center of the head, between the 2 physical eyes (past and present), the third eye focuses on the future, ignoring worldly distractions and transcending to a higher realm of consciousness.

## An Imbalanced Ajna

An imbalanced Ajna disconnects us from our true selves with an increased hunger for material things and an emphasis on negative thoughts and troubles of the past that cause it to be blocked. According to a French philosopher, the Ajna is connected to the pineal (the seat of the soul) and pituitary glands. If the Chakra's energy flow is moving downwards, that usually suggests an imbalance of sorts, with signs of feeling angry, irritable, depressed, and self-limiting beliefs. The third eye's imbalance causes this psychological toll. A physical sign of imbalance usually appears in the form of headaches, eye problems, brain disorders, and poor memory.

## Healing the Imbalance

To heal the third eye, start with visualization. This goes nicely with:

- Meditation
- Aromatherapy
- Adding purple to your wardrobe
- Listening to classical music
- Yoga
- Affirmations
- Sun gazing
- Breathing techniques

## The Crown (Sahastrara Chakra)

The final Chakra, known as the Crown or Sahastrara in Sanskrit, meaning "a thousand petals," is the highest Chakra guiding us to the supreme self, connecting us with the universe's cosmic energy. If you are connected with your inner self and find purpose beyond the material world, know that these are signs the wheel is spinning efficiently.

A healthy Crown Chakra usually translates into a healthy spiritual existence.

The energy emitted from this Chakra has a sense of cleanliness and clarity, like a breath of fresh air.

## Characteristics

The Crown's element is thought or, in some scriptures, cosmic energy. Other teachings suggest there is no element associated with it at all, that the Crown is pure spirit, transcending the physical form to flow freely.

It is said to be represented by three colors, gold, white and purple. These colors connect us to the higher self, signaling a focus on spirituality, adapting profound change, and shedding the material realm.

Its symbol is the thousand-petaled lotus, that symbolizes the divine and the infinite. It is shown as a picture of the divine circle within the lotus, which points to a connection with the Hindu God of creation, Brahma.

## Location

The Sahasrara sits at the top of the head, governing the brain and nervous system.

## An Imbalanced Sahastrara

An overactive or underactive crown Chakra can influence the brain's memory and focus.

This has a negative effect on the mental and physical health associated with the Crown, showing up as a disconnection from your inner self, lack of inspiration, lack of focus and confusion, emotional blockages, imbalance, head pains, or sleeping problems.

## Healing the Imbalance

The Sahastrara energy is closely connected to the other six Chakras. Therefore, to allow energy to flow freely and release the blockages, you have to work on healing the first six Chakras along with the Crown. While doing so, you can adapt a few of the following practices:

- Meditations
- Yoga
- Affirmations
- Physical movement
- A regular sleep schedule
- Detoxing and fasting
- Organic and fresh foods

# Chapter 3:

## Healing and Balancing Chakras

Balancing and maintaining a healthy Chakra can contribute to all aspects of our lives. Maintaining healthy relationships, mental and physical balance, and emotional stability are all signs that our wheels of energy are spinning in the right direction with the right speed.

Let's take a closer look at some of the ways to balance, unblock, and cleanse our troubled Chakras.

### Root Chakra (Muladhara)

**Movement** - Exercise and dancing are effective ways to reactivate the blocked energy flow; whether you can dance or not, it's the rhythmic movements that allow for a closer connection and a feeling of comfort in your own body – even a walk can help in cleansing your Chakra.

**Meditation** - Indoor or outdoor meditation is a surefire way to restore your energy levels. Picturing the color or symbol of the set Chakra at the end of your spine and visualizing its expansion towards earth will ground you back in place.

A body scan meditation in which you lie on your back in a relaxed position moves your awareness through the different body parts so you can experience the different sensations without any judgment. Here you acknowledge any pain or tightness and keep breathing through it, accepting it, and imagining it, leaving the body on the out-breath and moving on to the next part of the body – working your way up from the feet to the top of the head.

**Yoga** - You can hold the tree pose, emphasizing your connection to your roots, by placing your left leg in a half lotus position and raising your arms to the sky while engaging your core for around eight breaths, making sure to switch sides.

**Breath work** - This includes diaphramic breathing, box breathing, pursed lip breathing, alternate nostril breathing, and 4-7-8 breathing.

**Food** - Nurture the body with root-based veggies such as carrots, beets, nuts, beans, and potatoes.

Eating red foods such as tomatoes, red apples, strawberries, pomegranates, raspberries, and the like nourishes the Chakra.

**Affirmations** - Using positive affirmations, whether during meditations or throughout the day, will give you focus. These affirmations include:

- I am safe
- I am rooted, grounded, and stable
- I am calm and content
- I let go of doubts, worries, and fears
- I love and trust my body
- I belong here

**Reconnecting with Nature** - Walking barefoot on the grass can go a long way in stabilizing your health.

## Sacral (Svadhishthana Chakra)

**Yoga** - A focus on the hip and lower abs helps with energy release. Hip opening stretches like the butterfly pose are among balance restoring exercises (start in a seated position with your feet held together – picture praying, but instead of your hands, use your feet – hold your feet with your hands, moving forward towards them until you feel your back slightly stretching. Hold for around 30 seconds while holding your breath, then exhale and repeat three times).

**Food** - I am happy to declare that, again, food is a factor in healing your out-of-whack energy wheel.

It is easy to match food with our healing process. In this case, with the first Chakra, we turn to orange-colored foods like sweet potatoes, carrots, mangos, and butternut squash; go crazy with your choices. Just avoid any artificial coloring – Cheetos don't count as healing foods.t

## Affirmations

- Life is pleasurable
- I deserve pleasure in my life.
- I move easily and effortlessly
- I absorb information from my feelings
- I embrace and celebrate my sexuality

**Journaling** - The therapeutic process of writing your emotions down on paper helps start your healing in this Chakra and your understanding of the turmoil and doubts within. Journaling connects you with your inner self and puts things into perspective in the physical world.

**Meditation** - Visualization meditation is one method of meditation that helps restore balance. Place your main focus on your breath until you find a steady rhythm. Once you've secured your focus, picture a body of water – a lake, a stream, or the ocean – and hold that image in your mind while maintaining a steady breath for several minutes.

## Navel/Solar Plexus (Manipura Chakra)

**Yoga** - Since fire is this Chakra's element, the Sun salutations are the most appropriate poses to go with.

**The classical forward bend** – sitting on your Yoga mat with your legs extended together or hip wide apart, sit high on your sitting bones, and inhale as you raise both arms towards the ceiling until they are in line with your ears. Exhale and bend forward, reaching for your toes with your hands, bringing your nose to your knees. If you sense any discomfort, hold your ankle, knees, or shins instead of your toes.

This straightforward pose can be performed along with the bow pose, seated spinal twist, and the warrior pose.

## Meditation

Meditation resolves almost all of the energy blockages.

There are several techniques to achieve balance. One that stands out is the Navel Chakra meditation technique. To do this, prop your back up with pillows and hold the position for 30 minutes without any discomfort while keeping your focus on the Navel area.

## Affirmations

- I honor the power within me
- I don't seek the approval of others
- I am ambitious and capable
- I feel ready to face challenges
- I am open to new ideas
- I forgive myself for past mistakes and learn from them

## Burning Incense and Oils

Burning saffron, musk, sandalwood, ginger, and cinnamon has the capacity to ignite our personal power.

## Reflecting on the Past and Healing from It

The past is in the past. That is not true for a lot of people – many of us store our past traumas in our bodies, which continue to affect our day-to-day lives. Going to therapy, seeking support from loved ones, and engaging in healthy habits helps in healing the fire, Chakra.

**Ingesting yellow-colored foods** - If it's yellow, eat it! Lemons, passion fruits, bananas, etc. Indulge yourself in any natural yellow food you can get your hands on.

# Heart (Anahata Chakra)

**Breathing** - Since the element of this Chakra is air, it is fitting that one of its healing practices is breathing, specifically the 'pranayama practice.' Inhale through the nose and exhale through the mouth for three to five counts each. Start with 3 minutes a day and increase according to preference.

**Yoga** - Upward-facing dog and camel poses are among the most effective Yoga poses to heal the heart.

**Green Foods** - When in doubt, EAT! Leafy greens such as spinach and kale, avocados, broccoli, and drinking green tea play an important role in correcting your connection with the Anahata.

**Affirmations**

- I am full of gratitude for my ability to love
- I feel compassion for myself and others
- My heart is open to receive love
- I am a conduit of love and peace

**Aromatherapy** - Burning scents such as rose, lavender, sandalwood, orange, and jasmine reawaken one's capacity to love

## Throat (Vishuddha Chakra)

**Food for throat** - apples, plums, and whole grains.

**Meditations** - Five minutes each day of mindful meditation can do wonders. It helps to visualize the light color of blue in your throat and connect with the right energy wheel.

**Yoga** - The shoulder stand and plough pose are two Yoga stances that cleanse the throat, Chakra. They reduce stress and pacify the nervous system, which enhances blood flow to the lungs, improving your breathing.

## Affirmations

- I let my voice be heard
- I listen to my own inner knowing
- I do no harm with my words
- I speak with authenticity, grace, and courage.
- I speak my truth.

**Neck and head stretches** - Making sure your neck is aligned with your spine is key, especially when practicing Yoga poses. Start by sitting or standing with your spine straight, drop your chin to your chest, and move your head to the left. Hold for 30 to 60 seconds and then move your head back to your chest and repeat on the other side. Repeat until you feel your muscles relaxing.

# Third Eye (Ajna Chakra)

**Meditation** - Visualize an indigo wheel in the third area, spinning and turning, removing all blockages and harmful flow of energy in its way.

**Aromatherapy** - Jasmin, Roman chamomile, nutmeg, bay laurel, myrrh, and sandalwood.

**Adding purple to your diet** - Grapes, chocolate, blueberries, and flavored tea are recommended. Incorporating vitamin D, cilantro, and raw cocoa helps in detoxifying the pineal gland.

**Yoga** - Downward dog, plow pose, and child's pose all align with the third eye Chakra and support the well-being of the soul and mind.

## Affirmations

- Ego doesn't cloud my thinking
- I can manifest my vision
- I have clarity in my thoughts
- I am open to my inner wisdom

**Sun gazing** - Do not do this at noon. Sun gazing is recommended either during sunrise or sunset when the rays aren't as direct or harmful to the eyes. It is considered a form of meditation to boost energy and enhance clarity of the senses and mind.

# The Crown (Sahastrara Chakra)

**Meditations** - Sit upright in a crossed-legged position or lay on your back in the Savasana pose. Focus on your breath, in and out. Observe your thoughts as they come and go without dwelling on them, detach yourself from them, and watch as a spectator like they belong to someone else, and then let them go.

**Yoga** - Poses that open up the Crown Chakra are usually inversion poses since the Crown is at the top of the head, such as Lotus, eagle, Rabbit, reclined bound Angle pose, and a headstand.

## Affirmations

- I am pure light and love
- I connect easily with spirit
- I am in clarity of my inner knowing
- I have access to wisdom and peace
- I am connected to the universe and to everything around me

**Essential oils** - White lotus flower and Chinese rice flower.

**Education** - Reading and listening to podcasts promote self-development. Expanding your knowledge and awareness, challenging the status Quo, and casting our limiting beliefs away, making room for a deeper understanding of the universe and our inner beauty.

**Detoxing and fasting** - Your spiritual self doesn't need food as your physical self does. Unlike the rest of the energy wheels, the crown chakra is best restored through fasting. This helps clear the mind and detoxify the body. Yet when it comes to food, the most beneficial are veggies, fruit, and drinking lots of water.

Some of the aforementioned techniques might seem a bit challenging in application and a stressful practice at first, but it is much easier than you think. These tips can be easily incorporated in our daily lives, whether regulating breath, having a healthy and balanced diet, walking, reading, journaling your thoughts and emotions before going to bed, venting and seeking support from a friend, or listening to classical and relaxing music.

All of these are techniques that can realign and calm your energy centers. Starting with just one a day can make a huge difference. And just because something seems hard at first doesn't mean it won't get easier. Practice makes perfect!

# Chapter 4:

## Chakras and Physical Health

Have you been experiencing unexplained pains and aches? Are you feeling off your game – dizzy or nauseated? Or perhaps you've been feeling great, balanced, and in sync with your body but aren't sure why that's happening – what change did you make that helped with your overall health?

As mentioned in previous chapters, each of the 7 chakras is connected to a set of nerves and primary organs within our bodies. While these physical manifestations of the wheels of energy thrive when the Chakra is open, balanced, and healthy, they also tend to suffer when there is a blockage occurring or a misalignment in energy flow.

The imbalance is usually exhibited through pain and discomfort spread throughout the body, with each sensation corresponding to its own specific wheel of energy. Each energy wheel has its own techniques to relieve the discomfort.

## Root (Muladhara Chakra)

The Muladhara is tethered to the vital force responsible for all excretion tasks. That force is called the Apana Prana, which looks after the expulsion of toxins from the physical body.

The Root Chakra, as mentioned earlier, is situated at the base of the spine near the perineum. Its corresponding organs are believed to be the Adrenal glands and the anus, as it is believed to exist between the anus and the genitals by the pelvic floor or Coccyx.

## Physical Symptoms of Imbalanced Root

When the Red Chakra is blocked, the energy flow to the rest of the Chakras is disrupted. Symptoms include the following:

- Sleeping difficulties
- Weight fluctuations (gain/loss)
- Pelvic pain
- Dullness and a feeling of inertia
- Constipation
- Lower back issues
- Colon problems
- Arthritis

## Healing the Physical Self

Rebalancing the energy and linking with your physical self naturally requires physical activity. The Shaktidas adopted the belief that the simpler solution is the most effective. Whether it is taking a walk, tending to a garden, moving the physical body through running, Yoga, or exercise – or simply going outside in nature, along with maintaining a healthy diet – can put you on the path of healing the Muladhara.

# Sacral (Svadhishthana Chakra)

The force tethered to this energy center is Prana Vyana, which translates to "the Energy of Circulation" (food, water, and energy).

The Sacral Chakra's location is in the lower abdomen, right below the Navel. Though there is no scientific evidence, the physical organs believed to be associated with it are the kidneys, reproductive organs, and the bladder. Being represented by the water element, it controls a lot of the body's fluids.

## Physical Symptoms of an Imbalanced Sacral

As this Chakra is also in the lower part of the spine, it shares some of the physical discomforts with the Root

Chakra, such as Arthritis, lower back pain, and lack of energy. It does include a little more than that, however. These symptoms are triggered by overactivity or lack thereof and include:

- Kidney and spleen issues
- Anemia
- Hypoglycemia
- Premenstrual syndrome
- Joint and hip problems
- Ovarian cysts
- Urinary tract infections
- Sexual problems

## Healing the Physical Self

You can never go wrong with movement. No one ever got anywhere by staying where they are. Yoga is always a top choice; however, since this Chakra element is water, a more tailored and effective solution would be to reconnect with water. Whether it's taking a shower or a bath or going swimming in a lake – or even your local swimming pool as long as you are near water – listen to water sounds or gaze out at a body of water during your meditations.

Eating food that is rich in healthy fats, such as fish, nuts, sesame, and sunflower seeds, helps in reawakening your Svadhishthana.

# Navel/Solar Plexus (Manipura Chakra)

The third force on our list is the Samana Vayu or the Samana Prana, which is the energy of digestion. As this Chakra is placed above the Navel all the way up to the rib cage, the associated organs include the stomach, small intestine, the pancreas, liver, gallbladder, and the adrenals. Yet it is mostly focused on the liver.

## Physical Symptoms of Imbalanced Solar Plexus

As this Chakra is located in the upper abdomen, the most common scenario of a physical ailment and health problems is digestive issues. The symptoms could occur in the case of an underactive Manipura, and they include:

- Nausea
- Eating disorders
- Feeling tired
- Indigestion
- Ulcers
- Heartburn
- Diabetes
- IBS
- Liver, colon, and pancreas issues

## Healing the Physical Self

To rebalance the Fire Chakra, you can probably guess the first method: YOGA. Breathing practices to regulate the energy flow coupled with meditation steadies the Manipura.

## Heart (Anahata Chakra)

This energy wheel is responsible for storage and distribution – otherwise known as Prana Prana. The Anahata is located, as mentioned before, near the heart at the center of the chest. This aids its corresponding organs, the heart, the lungs, circulatory system, shoulders, upper back, and, last but not least, the thymus glands. Most of these organs are closely attached to the element of this Chakra, which is (in case you need a refresher) air.

## Physical Symptoms of Imbalanced Heart

Signs of an unstable Anahata are closely linked to the organs it represents. In this case, they include but are not limited to:

- Breathing difficulties/asthma
- Immune system deficiency
- Heart palpitations

- Poor circulation
- Angina
- Upper back pain
- Blood pressure (high or low)

**Healing the Physical Self**

Eat leafy greens. Aside from the color coincidently being the color of the Chakra, greens are associated with heart health in general, and studies even show they could lower the risk of heart disease.

Yoga and meditation are perfect for this Chakra as they are all about managing and calming your breathing, and to accentuate their effects, it wouldn't hurt to burn some incense like jasmine, lavender, and Geranium.

## Throat (Vishuddha Chakra)

The 5th and final force is Udana Vayu, which commands the throat center. Udana means the upward-moving breath. Thisprana is also responsible for guiding the flow of energy from the lower Chakras to the higher ones. As established earlier, this Chakra is based at the center of the larynx, in the base of the throat. This also covers the thyroid gland, mouth, jaw, tongue, pharynx, neck, palate, and shoulders.

## Physical Symptoms of Imbalanced Throat

When the throat Chakra is out of balance, you may find it a bit challenging to communicate effectively. Among the physical signs are:

- Laryngitis
- Mouth ulcers
- Thyroid issues
- Sore throat
- Raspy throat
- Asthma

## Healing the Physical Self

Physical movement, specifically neck stretches, can alleviate a lot of the discomfort caused in the Vishuddha. Moving the neck from side to side, in a circular motion, or forwards and backward in a steady and slow motion to avoid injury helps in relieving stress from that area. Breath work alone, or incorporated through Yoga and meditation, can assist in the healing of this energy center as it is linked to the function of delivering the breath to the rest of the body.

Always keep the neck in line with the spine through correct body postures to avoid any hyperextension or strain.

Last, eat food that grows on trees, such as oranges and apples, as they are connected with the Vishuddha.

## Third Eye (Ajna Chakra)

As you may recall, this Chakra was located at the center of the head, deep within the brain, right between the brows – focusing mainly on the brain functions. The central organ of this particular Chakra is the pineal gland. This is responsible for the receiving and conveying of information regarding the current light/dark cycle from the environment, using light and melatonin secretion.

## Physical Symptoms of Imbalanced Third Eye

An overactive or underactive third eye can result in sensitive physical consequences. As it's placed in the center of the brain, near a cluster of nerves, the resulting impact from an imbalance can be rather disorienting. These consequences include:

- Insomnia
- Brain disorders
- Eye issues
- Headaches
- Neurological disorders
- Migraines

- Endocrine imbalance
- Disorders in the pituitary and pineal gland, hypothalamus

## Healing the Physical Self

Balancing the Ajna requires a great deal of patience and perception. Depending on the state of the imbalance, one can factor in the right procedure. If we're dealing with an overactive Ajna, it can be grounded through re-connecting with nature, bringing serenity, and dialing down the overactive waves in the brain. If we're dealing with an underactive Ajna, meditation is how to refocus and refresh the energy.

Starting a journal of our private thoughts can also help in increasing one's connection with their surroundings.

Yoga, specifically the headstand (Shirshasana), activates the Ajna and improves brain performance, along with other sensory organs around it.

## The Crown (Sahastrara Chakra)

This is the last and highest Chakra on the spine and energy flow. Being at the very top of the head, it shares organs with the third eye – mainly the pituitary gland, then the pineal gland, nervous system, brain, and hypothalamus.

## Physical Symptoms of Imbalanced Crown

When this Chakra is performing below its required level, it takes a toll on brain activity which, in turn, affects the rest of the body.

These side effects include:

- Chronic tension headaches
- Poor coordination
- Confusion
- A need to oversleep.
- Sleeping disorders
- Exhaustion
- Difficulty concentrating
- Brain fog
- Imbalance

## Healing the Physical Self

There are multiple ways to go about healing the Sahastrara and restoring balance. As most practitioners believe that the Crown is a doorway to the spiritual world, a lot of healing solutions include spiritual connectivity.

Meditation reconnects you with the body and opens up the mind to receiving information from the outside. Since it is all about self-awareness, being grounded in the moment, and maintaining a steady breath, it helps ease the Crown into a calm state.

Cleaning up the area where you reside and decluttering is key to physical and psychological health. Letting go of the hoarding mentality and embracing simplicity and minimalism can do wonders. Going through your home – one room at a time – will make the process easier and organized and give you milestones to celebrate after each cleanse.

Reading and learning about things is a different kind of meditation. Not only is your brain disconnected from distractions, but it's also being periodically nourished with information and expanding with each page you conquer.

Prayer is an effective method to open up the Crown. Not necessarily performed in a religious way, but rather a bridge to raising your consciousness and having a deeper connection to our astral existence.

In short, Chakras are not only about the spiritual and unseen energies. The approach to healing is not dissimilar to the health and lifestyle advice one would receive from a physician – from a healthy sleep schedule to balanced meals. Exercise, breath regulation, and an extracurricular activity performed on a warm summer's day outdoors are lifestyle choices recommended by doctors.

Balancing your Chakras to maintain your physical being doesn't require you to be an advanced Yoga practitioner. On the contrary, all you need is to be mindful of what your body is asking of you and take it day by day.

# Chapter 5:

## Chakras and Emotional Well-Being

In many ways, the 7 chakras influence and collectively participate in your emotional and mental well-being. Since the belief is that they exist primarily in the astral body rather than the physical one, it only makes sense that their impact is first felt within.

When the energy spheres are aligned and in sync and their flow is stable, people usually experience balance in their personal relationships and psychological well-being. A person would usually feel confident, content, calm, and in sync with their inner and spiritual self. You'll also be less judgmental of yourself and open to receiving positive energies and ideas to expand your horizons.

If the Chakras are unsteady, however, or their vibration sequences are not up to par, they may cause or increase the intensity of existing mental health issues, such as depression, low self-esteem, trust issues, and an overall pull towards the unpleasant.

As with the physical side of the chakras, there are methods to alleviate and stabilize the emotional and mental side effects of an imbalanced energy flow.

## Root (Muladhara Chakra)

The first of the 7 chakras is the base of the flow and the first energy wheel to look at when trying to re-align the rest of them. As its namesake suggests, this Chakra is responsible for feelings such as being rooted to the ground, stability, strength, and an overall sense of abundance.

The color of the root chakra is closely related to the instincts of survival, livelihood, and self-preservation, and the ability to hold up in the face of adversity and challenges.

## Emotional Symptoms of Imbalanced Root

The Muladhara is usually believed, among scholars, to carry within it generational traumas, wars, famine, and artificial and natural disasters, which create behaviors in our lives that could affect the energy flow.

One's childhood experiences can affect the way the root chakra performs, and the security that is often missing from our lives has little to do with what one is going through today and more to do with the sum of these lived childhood experiences.

These types of emotional and mental influences include:

- Nightmares
- Anxiety disorders
- Eating disorders
- Quick to anger.
- Lack of motivation
- Being self-conscious around others
- Controlling your surroundings
- Poor focus
- Depression
- Low self-esteem and self-pity
- Hoarding behaviors
- Greed

## Healing the Emotional Self

In healing the inner self, you will find that some physical methods also apply to the emotional unbalance. So, to spare you the repetition, we will focus on the more spiritual methods in healing here.

Among these methods are crystals, Yoga, and sounds.

The crystals that often affect the Muladhara include the bloodstone, the red jasper, and the garnet. Whether you place them on the general location of the Chakra while meditating or in the surrounding area of your home, they usually do the trick.

Sound and music play a role in harmonizing the body as well as chanting the mantra sound that corresponds to the root, which is "LAM." This can be done by itself or during the practice of Yoga.

As mentioned before, Yoga is a top contender when it comes to healing techniques; some of the poses that assist with the realignment include the mountain pose, the warrior two, the garland pose, the lotus flexion, and the half-bridge pose.

## Sacral (Svadhishthana Chakra)

The second Chakra on our list is mostly concerned with the overall sexual and creative well-being. This allows you to have new experiences, increase the sensations of joy and pleasure, express your emotions creatively, and like its element, water, it has the ability to transform and flow to adapt to the surrounding circumstances.

It also cultivates healthy emotions and connectivity to your inner child, along with stable relationships with partners.

Energy flows to and from the Sacral Chakra, allowing you to feel stimulated and dynamic while promoting sensuality.

## Emotional Symptoms of Imbalanced Sacral

The emotional downside of an unbalanced Svadhisthana takes many forms and shapes. Among those are:

- Fear of pleasure
- Loneliness
- Lack of creativity
- Anxiety
- Detachment
- Repression
- Trouble with emotional and sexual intimacy
- Emotional instability
- An overwhelmed feeling
- Addictive behavior

## Healing the Emotional Self

Working with the color orange is key in the healing process. When choosing crystals to focus the energy, the go-to rocks are the Carnelian crystal, eye of the tiger, orange calcite, citrine, and amber.

Sound is your friend, and this Chakras mantra is "VAM." Repeat at your leisure in meditation or Yoga.

Another healing method that hasn't been talked about enough is a variation and a close cousin to Yoga, "Mudras." Each Chakra has its own set of Mudras, just like they have their own set of preferred Yoga poses. A Mudra is a hand gesture usually displayed while practicing Yoga. Three of the most common Mudras for this Chakra are the Shakti Mudra, the Ksepana Mudra, and the Yoni Mudra. To perform them, sit in a crossed-legged position, monitoring your breath with a 4-count inhale and exhale, bring your palms together, interlacing your fingers, and release your index fingers. Then bring your hands in front of your pelvis and point the index fingers downward.

## Navel/Solar Plexus (Manipura Chakra)

The Manipura is associated with our inner power, will, and ego. This is the energy center of being assertive, having a strong sense of self, and having wisdom for decision-making. It guides us in having a life purpose and a deep understanding of our place in it.

### Emotional Symptoms of Imbalanced Solar Plexus

Mental and emotional symptoms of irregular energy to and from the Manipura include and are not limited to:

- Power-hungry and bossy
- Aggression
- Victimizing oneself
- Lack of confidence in one's ability
- Stubbornness
- Self-centric mentality
- Fear of rejection
- Negative thoughts

## Healing the Emotional Self

Another Mudra example is the Rudra Mudra which opens up the Manipura – this gesture symbolizes strength. Extend your middle and pinky fingers and bring your index and ring fingers to touch your thumb. While it is recommended to start with the Rudra if you're looking for another variation, the Matangi Mudra is slightly more complicated to perform, but all you need to do is interlace your fingers while bringing the palms together and pointing the middle finger upwards with the tips touching.

The gems associated with this Chakra are amber, yellow tourmaline, rutilated quartz, and topaz.

The sound associated with the Manipura is "RAM."

# Heart (Anahata Chakra)

The Anahata is all about forgiveness, gratitude, and love. It is your bridge between the 7 chakras and the middle point of emotional stability. It also represents attachment and unconditional love — not only to people but also to animals and other meaningful beings. Attachment, in a lot of cases, however, tends to rear its ugly head on occasion – being a double-edged sword, it could cause more damage than good. Whether that is to people, habits, or even food, attachment or detachment can sometimes disrupt our energy flow.

## Emotional Symptoms of Imbalanced Heart

Experiencing emotional pain in a heart chakra sounds almost poetic. Heartache is a well-known term, and the symptoms you may experience are:

- Commitment issues
- Issues with accepting and giving affection
- Shyness
- Antisocialism
- Disconnection from others
- Judgmental attitudes
- Lack of self-love
- Codependency

- Being fearful

## Healing the Emotional Self

To heal the Anahata, use the Mantra associated with it, "YAM" (pronounced as "Yan-gm"). You can pair this with a Mudra of the heart chakra while seated in a crossed-legged position, such as the Hridaya Mudra (said to help release emotions and heartache). This starts with tucking your index finger at the base of your thumb, connecting the tips of your thumb with the middle and ring fingers, and pointing your pinky fingers outward.

To help with the effectiveness of these practices, add the gems of the heart in the mix (Rise quartz, rhodochrosite, malachite, aventurine, or jade).

## Throat (Vishuddha Chakra)

All the other Chakras convene to communicate who we truly are, our thoughts, and emotions through the Vishuddha. The throat chakra is all about communicating in a way that empowers and inspires.

This Chakra doesn't just connect through spoken words; it is linked to listening as well. If you're a bad listener, that will imply the Vishuddha is blocked, almost like it is in our anatomy – the throat and ear are linked together. If you're hurting in one, you're hurting in the other.

## Emotional Symptoms of Imbalanced Throat

When the throat Chakra suffers, communication suffers. We're not listening to our intuition or to others — you could even call it a language barrier. Among the symptoms of a throat energy disruption are:

- Aggression
- Feeling misunderstood
- Reluctance to sharing emotions
- Anxiety about speaking your mind and truth
- Struggle in listening
- General lack of communication

## Healing the Emotional Self

Crystals associated with balancing the throat and maintaining it are among the aquamarine, sodalite, blue topaz, and the lapis lazuli.

Pairing those up with meditation and the Granthita Mudra requires interlocking the fingers in the palms with the thumbs pressed against one another, then place your hand close to the Navel and repeat the Mantra "HAM."

A Yoga pose to include here is the Lion pose, which helps in releasing the trapped energy in the blocked parts.

## Third Eye (Ajna Chakra)

The Ajna is about our intuition, seeing the unseen, and making sound decisions. This Chakra helps you tap into your inner thoughts, future dreams, and ideas. It provides insight, wisdom, and clarity. When it is flowing in the right direction, pinning at the right speed, it provides a sense of bliss.

An interesting fact is that the third eye has been included in studies about the mentally unexplained phenomenon, such as telepathy and lucid dreams.

### Emotional Symptoms of Imbalanced Third Eye

When the Ajna is blocked, the third eye cannot see the true world, your inner self is blind-sided, and you don't know where you're going.

Evidence of the imbalance include:

- Pessimism
- Uncertainty
- Confusion
- Self-limiting beliefs
- Mood disorders
- Self-doubt
- Overthinking
- Close mindedness

- Lack of purpose

## Healing the Emotional Self

Journaling is a good way to clear the mind and unveil thoughts and deep desires one is often surprised they have. And as the subconscious is linked to the Ajna, keeping a dream journal is a strong start in clearing the third eye. If you feel stuck, try journal prompts to get the ideas flowing.

Breathing exercises help in calming the mind and connecting you with your inner self by focusing on inhaling and exhaling.

Repeat the Mantra for the Ajna "OM" during meditation/breathing techniques and place crystals such as sodalite, purple sapphire, and rhodonite on the location of the Chakra.

## The Crown (Sahastrara Chakra)

Our last and highest Chakra is in charge of spiritual connection and well-being.

Maintaining the healthy energy flow of this Chakra means you know who you are and are truly at peace with yourself and others. An added bonus is having a strong connection with the universe.

## Emotional Symptoms of Imbalanced Crown

When this Chakra is blocked, a lack of spiritual subjects and a disconnection of the spiritual self occurs.

You'll also be susceptible to other symptoms, such as:

- A foggy mind
- Self-destructive tendencies
- Apathy
- Confusion about your purpose
- Poor connection with the world

## Healing the Emotional Self

To heal the final Chakra, implement its Mantra, which is a silent "OM" or "AH" during Yoga poses such as the corpse pose, the rabbit pose, or the lotus pose.

You can throw in a Mudra such as the Mudra of the thousand petals, in which you connect the tips of the thumbs and the tips of the index fingers to form a pyramid. Then spread the rest of the fingers, pointing them upwards, and bring your hands above your head.

The crystals used to clear and stabilize the Crown are the moonstone, tanzanite, ametrine, and clear quartz.

A regular sleep schedule is key when calming the energy flow and balancing the Sahastrara.

As is with healing the body, one must pay attention to their emotions and psychological well-being. Your inner self sends you signals — and emotional pain in your heart or mind needs as much consideration as any physical discomfort you feel in your body. By maintaining a healthy mind and body, you'll be able to overcome any challenges in your way and come out the other side thriving.

# Conclusion

The energy wheels within our bodies are like a smoldering fire, dormant, yet alive, waiting for you to bring it dry wood so it can rage and spread warmth through our different beckons of Prana and awaken the rest of the body and consciousness with it.

As we start implementing the teachings of the 7 chakras, our energies will gradually move from darkness to light, bringing with it a new dawn to our senses and physicality.

Maintaining the flows of the Chakras within our bodies and just beginning to understand their significance and impact on our lives is a huge step forward to a life free of unexplained pains and aches. This will keep us safe from falling victim to mood swings and mental instability and pave the road to an enlightened start to spiritual ascension.

Some practitioners believe this journey can take several lifetimes, but that belief should not limit you in trying to break the odds. It's not a race — we each heal at our own pace and have different traumas and life lessons to learn from and work through. Just because someone achieved balance before you did does not mean you're failing. You might have a heavier weight to carry that requires longer to be uplifted. And while you might stumble along the way, it does not mean you're lost forever (x-men fans will relate). You can find your way the following day, week, or month as long as you try again!

Knowledge of this practice is believed to have primarily been passed from generation to generation through oral tradition and through the Indo-European people, also known as the Aryan people.

As most of the scriptures are lost in history or transferred through too many conduits, it is important not to consider any of the practices as an established fact etched in stone.

As with all things in life, you have to go through the process of trial and error to find what fits you best, what you find the most fulfilling, and what your body reacts positively to.

For some people, the practice of Yoga is not as satisfying as trying something more practical that fits their schedule, such as walking and exercising. Others prefer to meditate and use Mudras as they find connecting with their spiritual selves easier in solitude and silence.

It's vital to point out that not all that glitters is gold. Just because someone walks up to you saying they have the magic crystal that will heal your ailments, and provide you with a sense of rebirth, doesn't mean that they have your best interest at heart.

Do your homework, research, and look up what you need and then find tried and trusted resources to secure the tools for the betterment of your health.

Start with yourself — you can only help others find their balance after finding your own. You need to put your oxygen mask on first before helping others with theirs. And just as a medical checkup, make sure you have a chakra checkup periodically to maintain a healthy energy flow.

# References

*Blog*. (n.d.). Midtown Yoga Studios. https://midtownyogastudios.com/blog/

Energy Academy. (2022). *Third eye chakra: Healing therapy, fundamentals of chakra balance*. Energy Academy.

Jain, R. (2020a, August 26). Unlock the power of the Sacral Chakra: Guide to svadhishthana. *Arhanta Yoga Ashrams*. https://www.arhantayoga.org/blog/svadhishthana-chakra-all-you-need-to-know-about-the-sacral-chakra/

Jain, R. (2020b, October 8). Crown chakra: The divine energy of Sahasrara chakra. *Arhanta Yoga Ashrams*. https://www.arhantayoga.org/blog/crown-chakra-divine-energy-of-sahasrara-chakra/

Johnson, C. (2023, January 23). *Root Chakra description.*

Judith, A., & Yugay, I. (2022, September 27). *8 ways to heal your throat chakra*. Mindvalley Blog. https://blog.mindvalley.com/throat-chakra-healing/

Julia Childs Heyl, M. S. W. (2023, February 7). *What are the 7 chakras and what do they mean?* Verywell Mind. https://www.verywellmind.com/the-7-chakras-and-what-they-mean-7106518

*Latest articles - mindbodygreen*. (n.d.). Mindbodygreen. com. https://www.mindbodygreen.com/articles/

Lechner, T. (2019, October 9). *Chakra cleansing: How to clear your chakras & free your energy*. Chopra. https://chopra.com/articles/chakra-cleansing-how-to-clear-your-chakras-and-free-your-energy

Lindberg, S. (2020, September 21). *Throat chakra healing: How to unblock for better health*. Healthline. https://www.healthline.com/health/throat-chakra-healing

Love, & Relationships. (n.d.-a). *5 ways to open your heart chakra*. Goodnet. https://www.goodnet.org/articles/5-ways-to-open-your-heart-chakra

Love, & Relationships. (n.d.-b). *Chakra healing: How to open your crown chakra*. Goodnet. https://www.

goodnet.org/articles/chakra-healing-how-to-open-your-crown

*NAAD*. (n.d.). Naadwellness.com. https://naadwellness.com/chakras-spinning-the-wheels-of-soulful-living.php

Ness, K. (2018, February 22). *Heart chakra: Here's everything you need to know about your fourth chakra.* YouAligned™. https://youaligned.com/mindfulness/the-heart-chakra-how-it-impacts-your-ability-to-love-and-be-loved/

Opening the crown chakra. (2022, December 9). *Bettersleep.com.* https://www.bettersleep.com/blog/opening-the-crown-chakra/

Shah, P. (2020, August 20). *A primer of the chakra system.* Chopra. https://chopra.com/articles/what-is-a-chakra

Spitz, J. (2022, April 8). *3 tips to balance & cleanse your heart chakra.* The Detox Market. https://www.thedetoxmarket.com/blogs/news/tips-to-balance-and-cleanse-your-heart-chakra

Stokes, V. (2021, July 27). *Got balance? Try these chakra affirmations to heal with the power of words.* Healthline.

https://www.healthline.com/health/mind-body/chakra-affirmations

The Heart Chakra: Discover and balance the fourth chakra. (2020, December 30). *Art Of Living (United States)*. https://www.artofliving.org/us-en/meditation/chakras/heart-chakra-fourth

*The Sacral Chakra*. (2018, January 31). The Refinery. https://therefinerye9.com/the-sacral-chakra/

*Throat Chakra*. (2023, January 23).

(N.d.). Artofliving.org. https://www.artofliving.org/us-en/meditation/chakras/